About the Author

Sally Rawhey, published her first book, *The Unspoken Voices*, by Olympia Publishers in 2018. Her professional career always involved writing, from journalism, magazine editing, television programs script writing, ads copy writing to song lyrics and documentaries script writing. She has also worked as a Television Programs Director and Creative Director on different television channels in the Middle East for over a decade. Once again, Sally Rawhey wraps up her feelings into a series of poems in her second book, *There*.

There...

Sally Rawhey

There…

Olympia Publishers
London

www.olympiapublishers.com
OLYMPIA PAPERBACK EDITION

Copyright © Sally Rawhey 2020

The right of Sally Rawhey to be identified as author of
this work has been asserted in accordance with sections 77 and 78
of the Copyright, Designs and Patents Act 1988.

All Rights Reserved

No reproduction, copy or transmission of this publication
may be made without written permission.
No paragraph of this publication may be reproduced,
copied or transmitted save with the written permission of the
publisher, or in accordance with the provisions
of the Copyright Act 1956 (as amended).

Any person who commits any unauthorised act in relation to
this publication may be liable to criminal
prosecution and civil claims for damage.

A CIP catalogue record for this title is
available from the British Library.

ISBN: 978-1-78830-535-8

First Published in 2020

Olympia Publishers
Tallis House
2 Tallis Street
London
EC4Y 0AB

Printed in Great Britain

Dedication

To everyone who lit my heart with God's light…
Family, friends and strangers…

There

There...
Where enchanting moments are made,
where new smiles are engraved,
where pure feelings are painted.
There...
Where craved dreams are planted,
where weak determination is rooted,
where fresh ambitions are sprinkled.
There...
Where lovers' hearts meet for the first time,
where an unborn child is embedded
in his mother's heart,
where the gone unite after they depart.
There...
Where age is ageless,
where worries are seedless,
where fears are voiceless.
There...
Where God awaits you
love is created.

WORLD AT MY DEMAND

I was once too many;
had the ambition of a dozen,
possessed the will of a nation,
owned the dream of a tribe,
held the sun in one hand,
called all earth my land,
victorious with no victories,
the world at my demand.
My path was full of pitfalls,
yet above them I stand.

ESCAPE LOVE

I ran away from you.
Escaped the stare of your eyes,
kept between us a thousand miles,
climbed the highest mountains
and learnt to forget.
Roamed dangerous deserts
and buried the regret.
Dived below the deepest seas
and drowned the longing with ease.
I flew higher than birds could fly
and forcefully threw your love down from the seventh sky.
I erased your traces from my soul.
I successfully silenced your siren calls.
I ran away from you.
How did I end up at your door?

NOT YOU

Don't get all haughty,
you own nothing here.
The pretty face
may seize to be dear.
The riches you acquire
may become your greatest fear.
The friendships you made
may choose not to stay near.
The beliefs you long fought for
may no longer adhere.
The talents you proudly possess
 may one day disappear.
Don't get all haughty,
you own nothing here.

LOVE POTION

Give me a potion of love
and let me drink;
lose my head to it,
cease to think.
See the face of my love
with every blink.
Write mountains of letters
'til life runs out of ink.
Sail on seas of emotions
and willingly sink.
Step out of my old self,
lose every link.
Give me a potion of love.
Let life's ugliness shrink.

Piccadilly, Here I Am

I am not from this country,
a tourist I am.
I came to London with the biggest plan,
but a long list I was asked to get back
by my family and clan.
"Everything you find for fortnite, Mummy,"
was the wish of my youngest man.
"Hell with fortnite.
Why aren't you of school a bigger fan?"
Piccadilly, here I am.
Then my eldest asked for Messi new shoes,
55 sterling. Oh damn!
They say it's in a store called, 'Lilywhite',
you find under that brand.
Piccadilly, here I am.
My hubby had asked for that cable,
"a miracle!" he says. "It connects Netflix to dv cam."
Can't risk making our marriage unstable,
must gift the cord to my man.
Piccadilly, here I am.
My brother wants that history book:
only at main Waterstones branch
you can find. that same book he lost twice.
It's been his yearly demand.
Piccadilly, here I am.
The list beamed long and days grew short on me.

Piccadilly, my daily destination,
a bad dream I failed to foresee.
It seemed Piccadilly was a bad destiny,
that I couldn't flee.
I travel to visit London
and it's only Piccadilly I see.
So, I threw away the list.
No more Piccadilly, it's time for my spree.
Rushed to catch that musical I long longed to see.
I stopped the cab driver with a plea,
"Take me to the magic of theatre.
Take me away, I must flee."
But road by road, I felt the load.
The familiarity of the place sinking on me.
It's the Piccadilly Theatre.
Piccadilly, yet again, conquers me.

PRETEND

Pretend you're strong,
that you don't care.
But hide those falling tears
before they leave you bare.

Pretend you never loved,
that you don't have feelings.
But conceal the look of longing
before it manifests into meanings.

Pretend you're indifferent,
that you confidently assert.
But discard that bitter smile
before it reveals your hurt.

I AM BUT A LOVER

I am no atheist, no Buddhist, no Sufi.
I am but a soul that breaths Your air.
I am but one who treads behind Your light when I look
out for You.
My heart has stronger sight
when I bow down praying.
I am higher than the highest height
where nothing but You can be seen.
Where nothing but Your mercy
was ever meant to mean.
I am but a lover who chose a love,
greater than the conscious mind could ever dream.

AGELESS

Dye the white in your hair
or leave your wrinkles bare.
A beautiful heart worn with years,
only grows more fair.

WHY SO FAST?

Why so fast your little hand
grew to cover all mine?
When only just yesterday,
it was a tiny dime.
Why so fast
your small voice
became so rough and manly?
When only just yesterday,
it was the sweetness of candy.
Why so fast
the cute toddler face
morphed into this handsome cast?
When it was only yesterday.
Why couldn't it last?
Why so fast
my little boy is no more searching
for all his loved toys?
Why so fast
the little legs
stand now taller than mine?
Why so fast
the funny, childish face
became a teenager's cynical gaze?
Why so fast
you grew up on me?
Take a little longer

before your eyes say,
"Mama, set me free".
Your childhood was my blessing.
My arms still didn't get enough
of our long, long hugs.
My lips still didn't quench their thirst
of calling you all your pet names.
My pillow is still not ready
for you to desert it.
Stay young a little more,
before your friends fill my space,
before a beautiful, young girl steals your heart
and your feelings for her
takes you worlds apart.
Stay young a little more.
A lifetime in my arms
is still not enough.
I need more.

AND YET

Distances separate us,
deserts and streams.
Time separates us,
decades and years.
Days separate us,
ambition and dreams.
Yet you still want me
without any fears.

SAD EYES

She, who has the sad eyes
glittering with tears.
She, whose smile ties hearts
like ships are tied to piers.
She, who watches over her children
like a God-fairy of a million years.
She, who faces the winds
with so much strength.
Unaware of how she's admired
for all this strength.
She, whose laughter
beats the loudness of kids,
even when tears threaten to flood
her closed lids.
She, who stands now belittled by so much ill,
questioning silently and regretfully…
God's will.
Tell her,
pain is never meant to stay.
Tell her,
even the darkest, stormy clouds,
the sun will surely drive away.

AMBITION OR LOVE?

Are they for me,
the feelings I see?
Are they for the shine of my eyes,
the shape of my smile,
the move of my hair?
Are they for
the tone of my voice,
the feel of my presence,
the pace of my walk?
Are they for me
or for a life I own,
a job I perform,
a power I possess?
Success with no prior stress,
a status I can grant you.
A position I can put you through.
Are they for me,
these feelings I see?
Or for a life you believe achievable
if you climb up beside me?
What is it that you admire?
The shine in my eyes
or the shine of the stars?
If it's ambition that moved you,
you've rationalised the untrue.
I have nothing to give.

You'll waste the dream
you thought you'd live.
You'll find nothing in these eyes.
Even love can be wise.

SAY SHE WAS

And if I die today,
Don't search for me.
Say, 'She was but a soul,
then God set her free'…
She was a prisoner in between
blinding earthly needs.
Kind thoughts and mean,
like a knotted line of beads,
then God set her free…
She only saw the narrowness
of tomorrow.
She only feared her own sorrow,
for she was as human
as all things hollow.
Then God set her free…
She followed her kid's laugh,
like it's eternal.
She admired human beauty,
from the external.
She leaned on her parents,
like they're immortal.
Then God set her free…
Where there is no
here and there.
rich, famous or bare.
no youth, no truth,

no anger, no swear.
Where nothing stands tall,
but God's gracious face.
No humanly voice
all perishes, but God's grace…

NOSTALGIC

Nostalgia hits
to a promise once told
of a word.
I thought then, you'd forever hold.
But,
perhaps not.
Time passing and growing old,
still living on a fake promise,
you once told.

WINGS OR RINGS?

In this world,
I have seen people flying without wings,
and I have seen people chained without rings.

SPEECHLESS

If I'd to tell you how I love you,
I'd be speechless.
The world hasn't that much time;
I'd be breathless.
No language would say it right;
they'd be useless.
No description would give the worth
of your uniqueness.
No emotions could express the magnitude
of this deepness.
If I'd to tell you how I love you,
I'd spend my life sleepless.
With this immeasurable love,
expression is needless…

WALK AWAY...

They'll tell you
the skies are grey,
and the storm is inevitably
coming your way.
Just walk away...

They'll tell you
war is behind the door,
and misery will hit
crueler than ever before.
Just walk away...

They'll tell you
people will cheat you,
stab you from the back,
deceive you and defeat you,
Just walk away…

They'll tell you
love is just a mirage,
a blind man's dream,
a synonym of sabotage.
Just walk away…

They'll tell you
death is near,

beware and fear.
Alas you die with no one near.
Just walk away…

They'll tell you
they'll scare you.
They'll distract you
with words untrue,
but you can alter the worst fate,
if faith lives in you.
So, just walk away…

THE ANSWER IS 'NO'

You thought there was a chance,
that your smile can make his heart dance,
that you can be a part of his romance.
The answer is 'no'.
You thought he intentionally holds your stare,
that he searches for you everywhere,
that he made up interests for you to share.
The answer is 'no'.
You thought that he genuinely cared,
that bumping into him was all prepared,
that in spite of impossibilities he dared.
The answer is 'no'.
Pick up your scattered emotions and run.
Spare yourself the tragic show.
The answer is 'no'.

WHY DREAM AGAIN?

You dreamt a thousand dreams,
yet dared not to step in.
So why dream again tomorrow,
if you fear to grow wings to your skin.
Wait not for wisdom to lead you,
wasting your dreams is the greatest sin.

LISTEN WELL

Open your heart
and listen as I tell.
I will give you some wisdom,
so ponder on it well.
You're no longer the child who trod
with a flower in her hair.
Age has faded your colors,
you're no longer that fair.
You may not turn heads
with a glitter in your eyes,
your absence doesn't stir
admirers to agony or cries.
You may even pass unnoticed,
not followed by eyes.
So if it's beauty that shielded you,
beauty fades like clouds in the skies.
But if it's your heart's goodness,
it's a well that never dries.
People will forever need you,
to alter their bitterness with smiles.

BAG OF SINS

Here is my big bag of sins.
I've lied,
I've cheated,
I've done so much wrong.
I witnessed people's sufferings,
with a heart of stone.
I've talked bad,
I've stabbed in the back,
and I have hid it for too long,
in this very bag
I put it before you,
in front of Your door.
You promised by your mercy
to exchange it to good.
You said you'd forgive,
You promised You would.
For I have sinned
in confidence of your mercy.
Here I am,
acknowledging my mistakes
before You with curtsey.
Waiting to take my bag back empty,
clean of my guilt,
free of self-empathy.
White with your light
like a new heart unworn.
Like it never sinned,
like it's just been born.

IT'S ALL FAKE

Your love, your stare,
your eyes, your care.
The admiration so bare.
It's all fake.
Your smile, your time,
your poem, your rhythm.
The sweetness turned lime.
It's all fake.
Your look, your feel,
your silence, your appeal.
The whole lot is so unreal.
It's all fake.
How could I break?

BREXIT WITH TEA

I hate politics and politics hates me.
On my trip to Britain,
Brexit literally haunted me.
There's not a soul, a wall, a mall,
that the word doesn't echo in its hall!
Good Morning.
Brexit with coffee,
or Brexit with tea?
Or perhaps some Brexit with biscuits?
No thank you,
must take my Brexit spree.
It's getting Brexit late.
Are you Brexit mad?
Underground ad with Brexit stamped,
like it couldn't miss the word,
or mother Brexit would be sad.

FREE BIRDS

How beautiful are feelings
that know no age,
that race the winds like birds
freed from their cage.
How beautiful is desire
when it has no control,
when it willingly loses it all.
How beautiful the heart,
when it beats with madness,
dancing like a wild mare,
like it never tasted sadness.
Oblivious of the world's stare,
choosing surrender over sanity.
Nothing about love is fair.

OK I LIED

I acted like I didn't care.
I pretended I didn't notice
the hearty stare.
I pretended my presence
was just like everyone there.
I pretended the look you stole off me,
passed into thin air.
I pretended the hesitance in your words
wasn't there.
I pretended that ignoring you
was only natural and fair.
I didn't imagine my pretense
would leave me bare,
longing and dreaming
of one last stare.
I want your feelings
to surface once more.
Even if I pretend,
I never cared at all.

ONLY WHEN

When the green of your heart
mixes with the green of the fields.
When the weight of your thoughts
lightens like racing deers.
When the brown of your eyes
melts in the brown trunks of trees.
When the sound of your laugh
blends with the sound of the winds.
When the rhythm of your breath
morphs with the fluff of birds' wings.
When the pace of your steps
aligns with the tick of the seconds.
When the touch of your skin
becomes the feel of a petal.
When the drops of your tears
flood the rivers into waterfalls.
When the strength of your emotion
moves the waves of the ocean.
When your feet roam the earth
as easy as your heart flies the skies.
When you become one with all,
only then you are a free soul.

DIARIES OF THE BULLIED

A tennis court on a cold January night,
and a little girl in a grey dress, once white.
Jumping on a rope, careful not to be seen
by cynical friends, harsh and mean.
Hid in the shadows, hid behind screens.
Stepping from childhood to early teens.
Difficult the days, when stabbed and bruised.
Even childhood is a prison, when a child is abused.

A FOOL

Disappear,
like you never came.
You were just a fantasy
in my head.
A desire I failed to tame.
Leave no trace of your existence:
vanish, disappear.
Unleash the fear.
Let my heart rest,
you will be never near.
I was a fool
to disbelieve truth,
when it turned cruel.
Blow off this false flame,
if you wish to live sane.

WORDS FROM DAD

I saw his face between the clouds.
"Don't you remember me,"
he uttered not so loud.
"I was your dad, not many years ago.
I was the biggest love you had,
so why did your prayers stop coming,
replaced with meaningless humming?
Did you forget when I was long out of sight,
how I tucked you in every night,
or did my smile fade with time,
and other hearts replaced mine?
Maybe my absence
taught you to forget.
Maybe death
erased tears on a face no longer wet.
Smile and laugh,
my beautiful child.
Quench my thirst for you
like heavenly waters.
I still see you.
Death never blocked you though,
I see you so clear,
even from a different sphere.
All passes through
but not many prayers lately come from you."

WHAT, BUT LOVE?

What makes the soul shine with beauty,
with features unmatched and unseen,
with a look of grace
and a tender face,
that dazzles every passerby?
What paints the eyes the blue of the seas
or gives it the softness of growing leaves?
What colors the lips with shades of red,
more glowing than a fire's thread?
What gives it the splendor
that no one can resist?
What, but love,
defies all laws of logic?
What, but love,
enchants more than magic?

DON'T FEAR

Speak up,
don't fear,
even if the whole world is near.
Say you love me
in spite of it all,
the differences between us
are no barrier at all.
The levels between us
never mattered at all.
The distances between us
won't separate us at all.
Speak up,
declare you love me,
once and for all.

NOT YOURS

Did you think I was a bird,
free to choose,
that I take to the skies
with nothing to lose?
Did you think me free,
without ties or chains,
not owned by a past
of love and pains?
Did you think I was one,
not many more,
souls bond to my route
with no room for more?
Did you think me wanting?
Yes, true, I am.
I unconsciously long for you
but in reality, I can't.

BELIEVE

Your 'sick' will be healed.
Believe.
Your aspirations, long awaited, will be achieved.
Believe.
You'll be united eternally with all 'the loved ones'
gone. Believe.
Your sorrows today will be your blessings tomorrow.
Believe.
The Almighty promised.
Who, but a fool, would disbelieve?

I RAGED

I raged at the sun
that ruled second to none,
and hid its light when it wished.
I raged at the full moon
that shrunk too soon,
losing the battle of existence.
I raged at the tide
that abandoned little fish's side,
with the first hit of dry sand.
And I raged at the soft rhythms
that traveled invincibly to my soul.
I raged at the bold smell of roses
that enchanted my senses, in spite of it all,
I raged at the sweet dreams
that visited my sleep uninvited.
I raged at my heart
that signaled love with words unpredicted.
I raged at my will
that denied my legs the power to run,
and acknowledged a life of love more fun.
I raged.
I found no haven
but in anger.
I found no arms
but the wrath of thunder.
I was scared,

scared to replace my state of anger.
My eyes had befriended
the shades of black.
I feared to stray away
and lose my way back.
To be left blind
in the morning land.
A stranger imprisoned
in unfamiliar sand.
So, I raged.
I found myself weak before my needs.
I raged.
Alas, anger would verify my deeds.

INSANITY RULES

Your love for me
is illogical,
mad
and insane.
But who said
love
had rules
to its game?

NO TIME

Let this not be a day we waste,
with distance we enforce.
There will be so many days,
with distance we can't bridge.
There will be years of forgetting
and decades of erasing.
There will be too many things
to distract you from me;
like your wedding day,
the birth of your first child.
There will be so much in between,
like the other love you will find,
trips you will make,
relatives and friends,
the time you grow old
far from my eyes.
So why the distance
when you stand before me,
yet my legs can't take me to you?
Which of life's truths
make my closeness
a threat to you?

FROM YOU TO YOU

I strayed away.
Grab me back gently,
I have wronged.
Tell me it's okay, softly.
I have tried to hide from You,
 take me back mercifully;
for I've only hidden under Your skies,
I've only walked past Your miles,
I've only deserted You to Your seas,
took refuge in woods made of Your trees,
I've only ran away from You,
to You,
searched for myself everywhere.
Yet only found it
when I found You.

JUST A LITTLE SMILE

That little smile,
that passes between the world
like an arrow targeting my heart,
it landed on my soul.
My heart had closed its door,
but the soul has no limits
to keep you out.
The smile passed through.
I am involuntarily tied to you.

NO GAIN

"I've been listening",
I heard you say.
Back up now.
The words you are about to say
are not for you.
The feelings you are about to confess
are actually not true.
Back up now.
Before you lose your pride
and the tranquil waters
become a destructive tide.
Back up now.
Don't lose face
to the winds of pain.
Hide in your innocence,
this love is no gain.

WITHER

Why bother to bother,
when life itself doesn't bother?
What is sweet now,
will eventually become bitter
and what is young today,
will soon wither.

EVERYWHERE BUT THERE

See that far off island shore?
You walked with me there.
See that almost transparent cloud?
You held my hand there.
See these virgin corals far beneath?
You swam with me there.
See that high frozen mountain top?
We climbed together there.
See that distant, blue mirage?
We stood together there.
See the splash of North Pole penguins?
We played along them there.
See that tiny, dust powder star?
We lived centuries there.
You and I have been together everywhere,
but there.

NOT LAWFULLY MINE

It's the shameful truth
of wanting you.
Hiding it from the whole world
and unwillingly revealing it to you.
It's the shameful longing
that seeks your nearness,
that torments my soul,
leaving it heedless.
It's the shameful admiration
that comes with anticipations,
not lawfully mine,
feelings akin to a crime.
It's the shameful wanting,
not ending just starting,
exposing emotions
better dead not in motion.
If I could shoot this longing dead,
label it a sickness in my head,
but my heart is a traitor,
loving its own hater.

RISE ONCE MORE

What silenced your words
and dried their mist?
What blocked your rivers
and stopped their flow?
Isn't it about time you let go,
speak your heart,
let the world know,
that he who stands broken
will soon rise and glow?

WHATEVER IS

I don't know why
sorrow comes,
and burning tear drops fall.
But I know God is God
and watches over all.

I don't know why
we must part,
loved ones dear to our hearts.
But I know God knew why,
even before it all starts.

And so, in faith I believe,
regardless of the test.
No matter what each day brings,
whatever is, is best.

ALONE IS OK

Come out, little crab.
Don't fear the waves.
You're alone?
It's OK,
I too am the same.
You escaped the crowd,
feel no shame.
Revealing oneself
is a dangerous game.
Who said a happy life
needs fame?

I'M THE CREEP

Tell me your name.
I'm the creep.
I'm covered with lies and filth
so deep.
From where your fame?
From altering the truth,
the hatred and fear
that poisons youth.
Who gave you strength?
The sellers of guilt,
butchers of hope,
destroyers of all good built.

WILD

I want to speak all the languages
that no one still speaks.
Travel to Mars with a group of geeks.
Lead a riot to free birds from cages,
dance like a star on old Roman stages.
Dine in Delhi and sleep in Spain,
ride a stallion and race a train.
Be wild and wild be my name,
dare to play life's scariest games.
I fear not to change or age.
God created free souls,
it's us who built the cage.

BRIGHT IN BLACK

In the darkness
of starless skies
and the dimness
of deep, black tides.
Where vision perceives nothing
not even lights of distant cars.
In this pitch blackness I see **You** brighter than a million stars.

LIKE CRAZY

If I was simpler
and poorer,
you would have loved me
like crazy.
If I was less educated
and less sophisticated,
you would have loved me like crazy.
If I was just me
without the gifts
life gave me,
you would have loved me
like crazy.
But I can't be simpler,
I can't be poorer,
I can't be prettier,
I can't be cooler.
So, you can't ever love me
like crazy.

ONE & THE SAME

The broken chain,
the anger and the noble aim.
What made them taste the same?
Losing your mind
or finally sane?

HE IS HERE

God is here.
He doesn't hide
far closer,
than thoughts in your mind.
In the ringing of a church's bell,
in the reflection of water in a well.
In the sound of mosques' prayers.
In the clouds' massive layers.
In the loving call of a mother,
waking up her sleeping child.
In the warm pat of a father
silencing a kid, tearful and wild.
In a golden setting sun,
on a dark ocean tide.
In a blooming red rose,
coloring jungles in the wild.
Moses found his salvation
while drowning in the tide.
Jesus found him when from their betrayal
there was nowhere to hide.
Mohamed found him in the cave's darkness
and led humanity to the ultimate light, so wide.
God is here.
Don't search up the stars,
check in your heart.
HE'S only that far.

BEFORE IT'S PASSED

Capture the moment,
it passes so fast.
The blue of the waves
in your eyes won't last.
The feel of sweet breeze
on your eager face,
will fade into blast.
The little rays lighting the sea
will soon be past.
Capture the moment,
it will pass so fast.

I CHOSE YOU

From between all the world,
I chose you.
And, given the choice
I'd live it all again with you.
The wedding vows,
the giving births,
the good job.
The worst too.
The perfect car,
that ugly blue, too.
I'd live through the fights
and the happy, giggly nights.
The scattered clothes, the broken mugs.
The times we did the group hugs.
Nothing more soothing
than the warmth in your eyes.
More dear to my heart than a glittering sunrise.
I'd choose you from all the world's men.
I'd choose you all over again.

THE HAVEN

You are the escape
when sounds of life roar so load.
You are the refuge
when lost in harbours with wrong crowds.
You are the haven,
when hatred spreads like ashes in fire.
You are the truth,
when honesty has no buyer.
You are the light,
when hearts choose to go blind.
You are the lead,
when lies blur the mind.
You are the love,
when faith comes from trust,
You are the return,
when all else fades to dust.

LOVE STARE

Why did you look away,
pretend I am not there?
What is holding back
the love stare?
Was it the lie I said,
when I told them, I don't care?

DEFEATED

Pick up your weapons,
your shattered emotions,
your broken shield
and walk back home.
This love has defeated you,
vanquished you
and captivated your soul.
Life is not your salvation,
only God will make you whole.

YET YOU RETURN

And your feelings take you
to a younger sand.
Not your earth.
Not made for the touch of your hand,
yet you yearn,
yet you return.
To discover once more
that in this game of love,
you've passed your turn.

PIECES TOGETHER

Witness God that I love her,
and my heart finds a heaven in her heart.
Witness God that I wait for her
to put the pieces together,
when life scatters them apart.
Witness God that her presence
is a treat to my soul,
that ends when she departs.
Witness God that I see her
with no human form,
'cause our souls are paired from the start.

REFLECTIONS

I didn't realise I was aging.
I didn't notice
the shades in my hair.
My mirror was reflecting my inside.
So, I was often pitch black
and sometimes light and fair.

FROM BETWEEN

The two rocks will open
and waves will seep through.
I'll stand here in the middle
and my soul will climb up to you.
The skies will allow me
through to You.
Let me in.
I long for You…

TELL ME WHO?

Who is she,
whom your heart sings for?
Who is rocking your ships
and shaking your floor?
Who sails the winds of your thoughts?
Who leaves you sleepless,
longing for more?
Who do you follow
virtually and in real?
Who is she?
How does she feel?
How is it she stole your heart,
when I had its seal?

TAKEN

Will you now run,
that you know I'm taken?
Will you rage and cry
or were you simply unshaken?
Did you know all along
or was your judgment wrong?
Did you realize the forbidden,
or just playing strong?

THE PRAISE

Praise, like liquor,
can fog your mind,
blow your ego,
suffocate in you all what's kind.
So run from praise,
don't look behind.
If you taste its liquor,
true self may be hard to find.

THAT SMILE

Did you ever see the sun and moon
collide into one?
Did you ever watch heaven and earth
merge into one?
Did you ever view the sea and the sky
melt into one?
Did you ever witness night and day
become one?
I do…
Every time I see the smile of my son.

ON QUICKSAND I STAND

The foggy night cascades on my little car,
like an enemy seeking refuge in my womb.
A wavy road
beams before me a vacant lifetime.
It's my turn now to step on this sleek, velvety soil,
to grab my bottles of faith
and walk to the lethal sand.
The path before me became the goal once more.
Nothing changes.
No one utters a word,
they just sit and gaze as I walk back to you.
The mountains engrave me in a vacancy
filled with beaming eyes.
They think I'll lie and drown again.
They wait for the past to revive,
but I'll defy their laws of sanity.
I'll replant your seeds of happiness
in this burning soil,
I'll take my chances…
and throw the dice.
I'll gamble to stop the arms of the clock.
I'll stake to give away the freedom
that no one possesses.
I'll walk back to you.
Nothing scares me,
than to freeze forever in my spot.

To speak, and listen to my voice
echo back, unanswered.
I took sure, steady steps to the hollow land,
eager to hear your silky cries
seeping through the sand.
Tempting me, once again,
to abide by the rules of this land.
But life paves our paths,
when we chose to relive the mistakes of the past.
That's when day and night become one.
Light and darkness
are sometimes not related to the sun.
When you see the shallow gaps
between what was,
and what has become.
I walked to the valley of silence,
to that very dune
where youth has aged,
phantoms have sunk
and souls have disappeared.
I walked to the silky, yellow soil,
to the sleek, softness of its drops
that embraced many in its single hug.
I walked to the velvet earth
that hungrily calls for more souls.
I walked to the land of quicksand.
I walked to you.
Challenging its dormant, lethal pulls
and every eager victim under its soil.
I dared the yellow earth to cover my sight,
to swallow even the slight shortness of my height,

to become the master against my might.
I waited but nothing came.
Nature was a loser at its own game.
I knew I could walk 'til the end of the dune.
I knew I could freeze this softness to stone.
I fear nothing,
not even you.
You thought I'd stay out of your sand.
It needed a master and I became one.
I followed my own steps
and instinct led me to you.
Far and safe I hold you close to me,
the flesh and the sand.
The sound of your voice faded in the wind,
no pulse beats in your hand.
I had to cover you with quicksand.
Yet still! They sit and stare,
and sometimes they even dream.
The sun still sets in time,
leaving behind a conquered beam.
But I am no more the woman I used to be,
look in my eyes.
You won't see your smile in me.

IMAGINED ALL

Imagined feelings,
imagined warmth, imagined stares.
From a heart
that actually never cared.
Yet I imagine it all.
Alas, in my life
happiness plays a role.

FANTASIZE.

Want him as much as you want him.
He will never want you.
Fantasize as much as you fantasize.
It will never come true.
You centered him in your world,
but in his, there is no you.

FEELINGS LIKE WAVES

Feelings that flow with love,
can turn into monstrous waves.
Feelings that dazzle like sweet tides,
can alter into the seas' deepest caves.
Feelings that glitter like crystals on waters,
can shift into fatal shockwaves.
Feelings like waves have no rules.
They've enchanted and swallowed many fools.

JUST A LITTLE GIRL

I wish I was just a little girl.
I'd run into your arms and hide,
call your name a thousand times
without bothering you'd mind.
I wish I was just a little girl.
I'd stare endlessly in your eyes.
I'd hold tight your hand
and walk by you for miles.
I wish I was just a girl.
I'd wear your shirt and shoes.
I'd fall asleep on your lap
and cover up with your blouse.
I wish I was just a little girl.
I'd instantly tell you
I love you.
What has a little girl got to lose?

A MESSAGE HEARD

She told me,
that God told her,
the storm wouldn't stay.
The winds would die out,
the dust will fade away.
She told me,
that God told her,
the lights of her stage
will turn night into day
and crowds will cheer
as loud as they may.
She told me,
that God told her,
but little did I know
that she who breaths His love,
would find a full moon in a moonless day.

HEARTS OF NO RHYTHM

Mistake.
A crime,
loving a heart
that never loved mine.
Eyes of less feelings,
tears never shed.
Days unspent.
Sin.
A crime,
loving a heart
that doesn't rhythm with mine.
Feelings will die unsaid,
a love story that'll remain unread.

SO WHAT?

So what if you don't love me,
if you never wonder
what it would be like to have me?
So what if my smile
doesn't warm your heart,
if it passes unnoticed,
its ending like its start?
So what if you don't care
and never will,
if my well-being
is akin to my being ill?
So what if I come or go
and you don't care to know?
So what if you never had
an interest to show?
So what if you never did and never will admire me,
if I will always long for you silently?
So what?
You still bring happiness to my heart
and when you're gone
it won't hurt,
'cause we were always apart.

PATHETIC

A pathetic is someone…
Who sees 'no chance',
reads 'no chance',
yet still waits for 'a chance',
in a hopeless romance.

LIES

In all their smiles
I see the curve of your smile.
In all their eyes
I drown in the shade of your eyes.
There is nothing in them from you,
but I'm loving my own lies.

IMPOSSIBILITY

I may walk on a branch
instead of a leg.
Think with my fingers
not my head.
But avoiding my same mistakes,
remains an impossibility,
like raising the dead.

PARTICLES OF YOU

Wish there were other forms
'of you'.
Like liquid form
to quench my thirst.
I'd drink endless bottles
'of you'.
Or powder spray
to sprinkle on,
and feel billions of particles
'of you'.
Or in tablet shape
I'd swallow them all,
to sedate the painful longing
'for you'.
Wish there were other forms.
I'd get them all,
if I can't own the human form
'of you'.

A MIRACLE UNTOLD

It's been so long
that I heard your laugh
and I long for it.
It's been months and years
that I missed its ring
and the word 'hello'
that came from you.
How it moved mountains
and reconstructed them too.
The familiarity in your talk,
how I missed it so.
Its reliving was a miracle
to remain untold.
I have kept my distance,
 despite your silent calls.
I have kept far,
alas, all my defenses fall.

FROM UNDER THE UMBRELLA

I, the stranger
in the land of rain.
I, the roamer,
miles walked without pain.
From under the umbrella
I walk it through.
All signs will lead me,
all roads will get me to you.
From under the umbrella my face unseen.
Who cares who you are?
You're just another human being.
All the stories,
all the unknown glories
washed by the rain.
From under the umbrella
I stare at the unknown you,
London the city,
the haven of many who fled to you.
I have roamed your streets
searching for answers too.
I have come.
A visitor, a stranger, a seeker,
like many who rested on your floors
and searched for themselves in streets,
once the battlefield of many wars.
I, the nomad,

washed by your rain,
have fantasised. Myself, the Queen
with a crown, as glorious as a lion's mane,
and masses waving, almost insane,
awaiting a nod from me
but all in vain.
And I took lead in the greatest musicals
as I sat with the crowd,
sang along every song,
hit some notes others went wrong.
But the dream lingered
and the vision remained strong,
of a London dream,
that lingered in my heart for too long.

REGRETS

I, unlike many, have regrets.
Regrets of dreams I gave away,
of love words I didn't say,
of goodbyes uttered when I longed to stay.
I like many,
wish today was still yesterday.

SOUL PICTURE

If we post a picture of our souls,
how many would press 'like'?
Who would find it worthy of a comment?
What expression would they press:
love, wow or shock?

A ONE-SIDED COMBAT

Life did not break her,
she was too strong for that.
It was her own love
that thrashed her,
in a one-sided combat.
It fragmented her into pieces
so brutal, so fast.
She tried to survive it.
But for how long
can a shattered heart last?

DEAR LIFE...

Break my wings, I'll grow more.
Shatter my ambition, I'll restore it all.
Lock my dreams, they'll seep through doors.
Imprison me in fears, I'll blow up the walls.
Push me down your pits, I'll rise once more.
A heart shielded with God's love will survive it all.

CARE LESS

She didn't seek to be loved,
she didn't need the sweet speech,
she didn't care to be spoon-fed.
She never pretended she could preach,
She was hard with humanly flaws,
but in her heart God could be reached.

THE FINAL ACT

When gone, people will either tell
'She was of a good will'
or 'Her deeds were so ill'.
They'll either label me a saint
or a demon at hell's gate.
They'll count me among the pious
or a seeker of ugly chaos.
I'll either be a 'matter' to be told
or a 'nothingness' like mist in the cold.
Either this or that,
only my deeds
will write this final act.

Lightning Source UK Ltd.
Milton Keynes UK
UKHW010612200123
415672UK00005B/735